This Book Is For:

____

With Love,

____

BLOOM

PUBLICATIONS

Books That Help Kids Bloom & Grow

Your Future's So Bright We've Got To Wear Shades |
A Graduation Gift Book

ISBN:
979-8-9876827-9-1 - Hardcover

Illustrations by, Elina Oplakanska

First Edition, 2023
Bloom Publications

www.bloompublications.com

Your Future's So *Bright* We've Got To Wear Shades

A Graduation Giftbook

This Book is Dedicated to Graduates Everywhere

and Especially My 3 Amazing Kids
Collin, Allie & Joey

Celebrating their graduation years
SDSU - 2020
UCSB - 2023
TPHS - 2023

You can achieve anything you set your mind to!
With determination and action, follow your dreams, and I know
you will each positively impact the world around you and find
the success you are looking for.

With Love

Written in 2023

Cheers to you for a job well done!
We hope you learned lots, we hope you had fun!

We hope you made friends to laugh and to play
We're all here to celebrate you on your day!

You've learned so many lessons,
But it's important to know,

BE KIND TO YOUR MIND
H₂O
CAREER
YOUR LIFE the best ADVENTURE
friends
Enjoy Life
Life Master

Don't ever stop learning,
Continue to grow!
Be
Your Best
JOB
Lifelong Learning

Expanding your mind moves you forward in life
Even when obstacles sometimes bring strife.

How would you know what works the best,
If you never had struggles or never had tests?

YES
I made it around the roadblock! It wasN't so Bad!

So don't be afraid to stumble or fall.
A life without trying is saddest of all.

The things you will do, oh the places you'll see,
when you're trying your best, you'll be flying free.

Your mission in life is to
Find things you love.
When you focus on them,
Stars will shine from above.
Love Yourself
CHOOSE
HAPPY
SMILE
laugh
use your talents
Imagine

nternship
friendship
joy
DREAM BIG
Follow your heart
BE KIND
Do What You Want

You are smart, you are kind, you are talented too!
There's nothing in life that will be stopping you,

From giving your gifts, unique and rare,
Inside of you, there's brilliance to share.

So go out in the world and show them your best!
Think new ideas that you'll put to the test.

Sometimes Things Change...

New Date: __________________________________

How Have I changed since I graduated? ______________________

____

What new things have I done? ____________________________

____

____

How am I using my unique talents? ________________________

____

____

Where have I lived? ____________________________________

____

____

Where have I traveled? ________________________________

____

____

Big things I have already accomplished: ____________________

____

____

What is next for me? __________________________________

____